The Odd Squad's DISGUSTING Book for Boys

by Allan Plenderleith

BRRRR

RAVETTE PUBLISHING

THE ODD SQUAD and all related characters © 2007
Created by Allan Plenderleith
www.allanplenderleith.com

First Published by
Ravette Publishing Limited 2007
Unit 3, Tristar Centre, Star Road, Partridge Green, West Sussex RH13 8RA

ISBN: 978-1-84161-273-7

Is your lady bored of the '69' position?
Try the 99!

At work, make sure your secretary
backs up her stuff on a floppy.

When asking your lady to trim her beaver,
make sure she doesn't go too short.

What your **POO** says about you!

1.

YOU'RE A VERY GENEROUS, GIVING PERSON.
ALTHOUGH YOU GIVE SO MUCH IT LEAVES
YOU FEELING EMPTY INSIDE.

2.

A MESSY AND
IMPULSIVE PERSON.
WHEN YOU DECIDE TO
DO SOMETHING YOU
DROP EVERYTHING
AND GO!

3.

A SADO-MASOCHIST! YOU ENJOY PAIN
BUT YOU DO HAVE A TENDER SIDE.
(IE. YOUR TENDER BACKSIDE!)

4.  A REAL SNAKE IN THE GRASS! YOU'RE A SLIPPERY CUSTOMER WHO LIKES TO LEAVE NASTY SURPRISES IN LONG GRASS!

5.  YOU NEVER FINISH ANYTHING, ALWAYS CUTTING OFF JOBS HALF WAY THROUGH!

6.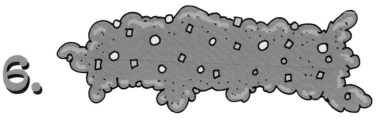

YOU'RE A VERY COLOURFUL PERSON WITH A CORNY SENSE OF HUMOUR!

7.

STINGY GIT.

Why naked cuddles by the fire are
not a good idea.

When checking out internet porn at work
be careful not to get caught.

How to avoid getting involved in
annoying family games of charades.

When suffering from 'man flu'
always make the most of it.

Make your own PORN MOVIE!

Costumes

MEN, WEAR THE FOLLOWING:
- HANDLEBAR MOUSTACHE
- BOILER SUIT
- CHEESY GRIN

WOMEN: WEAR AS LITTLE
AS POSSIBLE, PREFERABLY
RED AND SEE-THROUGH
(IE. STUFF YOU NORMALLY
WOULDN'T BE SEEN DEAD IN!)

Music

PLAY AWFUL, EASY-LISTENING
JAZZ MUSIC IN THE BACKGROUND.

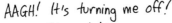

AAGH! It's turning me off!
Stop it!!

HAVE A SELECTION OF SEXY TOYS TO HAND.

 USE THE FOLLOWING SAMPLE SCRIPT AS A GUIDE:

```
Scene One - Front Door - Day

<DOORBELL RINGS>

HER:   Oh, HELLO there, handsome!!
       I'm all alone, you know!

HIM:   Hello Madam.  I'm here to
       fiddle with your pipes.

HER:   Ooooh yes, big boy! They're
       dripping wet.  I think you need
       to stuff something up them.

HIM:   Don't worry, I'll give them a
       good going over.  Why don't I
       pull out my big tool and
       get to work.

HER:   OOOOOOOOhhhh!  Tee hee hee!!!

<BONKING BEGINS>
```

Always keep your condoms away from the vicinity of pets.

When taking laxatives, never exceed the stated dose.

Demonstrate your skill in the sack to
the ladies by
simply buying a cream doughnut.

The best place for a dartboard is
not beside an open window.

Show your woman you love her -
buy her something with diamonds.

Don't be a typical bloke - now and again it's good to stop and ask directions.

On long journeys it's always a good idea to let the dog stick its head out of the car window for fresh air.

If, during sex, your lady begins tickling your bum, relax and enjoy it.

An important guide to BOGIE PICKING!

1. When going in for the pick make sure no-one can see you.

2. Pull bogie out slowly and carefully - but beware of attached nose hairs!

3. Wipe bogie discreetly under the arm of an armchair.

4. Alternatively use the roll and flick manoeuvre (can be dangerous).

Smuggling some dope through customs
is never a good idea.

Show your mates you're a real man by drinking like a fish at the weekends.

When picking your nose, it's never a good idea to go too deep.

Never visit your nan right after a fancy dress party.

When buying a new sofa always make
sure it's fire retardant.

Make sure you live longer by always eating 5 portions of veg per day.

Whilst your lady performs oral sex always beware of the gag reflex.

Show you're a real cool dude and
get into gangsta wrap.

To put the surprise back in your love life give your girl a golden shower.

During golf, make sure your ball never lands in a bit of rough.

Take the **BLOKE/GEEK** test!

(tick where appropriate)

If you're going to give a wedgie,
avoid ladies with g-strings.

Feeling stressed? Why not
hang out with your mates down the pub.

Why be uncomfortable during a long drive? If you need a wee just pull over and find a bush.

Don't embarrass yourself by scratching your bum in public - just find the nearest fire hydrant.

How to be a SERIAL FARTER!

1. For maximum impact, always blow off in enclosed spaces.

2. Blaming the dog does not always work.

3. To warn of silent but violent farts, insert a tiny whistle between your bum cheeks.

4. Always wear brown underpants in case of follow-through mishaps.

Whilst travelling on the sea, always be alert for possible dangers.

Never try to play your old records
on an iPod.

Beware of women who use tricks to get us to do the housework.

When playing with yourself,
make sure you lock the door.

A handy guide to getting PISSED!

1. Don't eat much before drinking - it just takes up valuable space!

2. Why stick to one drink when there's such a great selection!

3. You know you're getting nicely drunk when Mr. Johnson makes an appearance.

4. If you feel sick, whatever you do DON'T put your hand over your mouth.

When the missus asks you to bring home a juicy pear from the market, take advantage of her blunder.

To make round-buying simpler, put
your money in a kitty.

Make it your New Year's resolution
to lay off the fags.

Beware of sexual encounters with women
who haven't had it in a while.

<u>Secrets for an amateur CHEF!</u>

1. The best cooks always use generous quantities of wine.

2. After chopping chillies, always wash hands BEFORE going to the loo.

3. When using recipes, feel free to experiment with your own ingredients.

4. If everything goes wrong, secretly buy something in.

To experience a fun, free, spinning vortex simply stand between two old ladies.

How to tell if your cat is female.

Give your girl a treat and spend
all day deep inside her bush.

Give your lady a special lower back massage - no hands required.

If you haven't had sex in a while, release your frustration by spanking the monkey.

Whilst performing life-saving
mouth-to-mouth procedures, remember not
to blow too hard.

An idiot's guide to iPODS!

1. To prevent theft from chavs, simply wrap your iPod in a job offer.

2. Don't turn the volume up too high - you may not hear something important.

3. Never let it out of your sight in case your friends discover those embarrassing albums.

4. Always back up music files in case of accidents.

Beware of women who say they want a threesome.

Remember - women love a
good muff diver.

Always speak clearly when asking someone to check out your new spectacles.

What happens when you twiddle
nipples too much.

Why it pays to get a job near a nuclear waste plant.

When someone comes round collecting for the old folks' home - hide.

Fed up with chips?
Why not try onion rings?

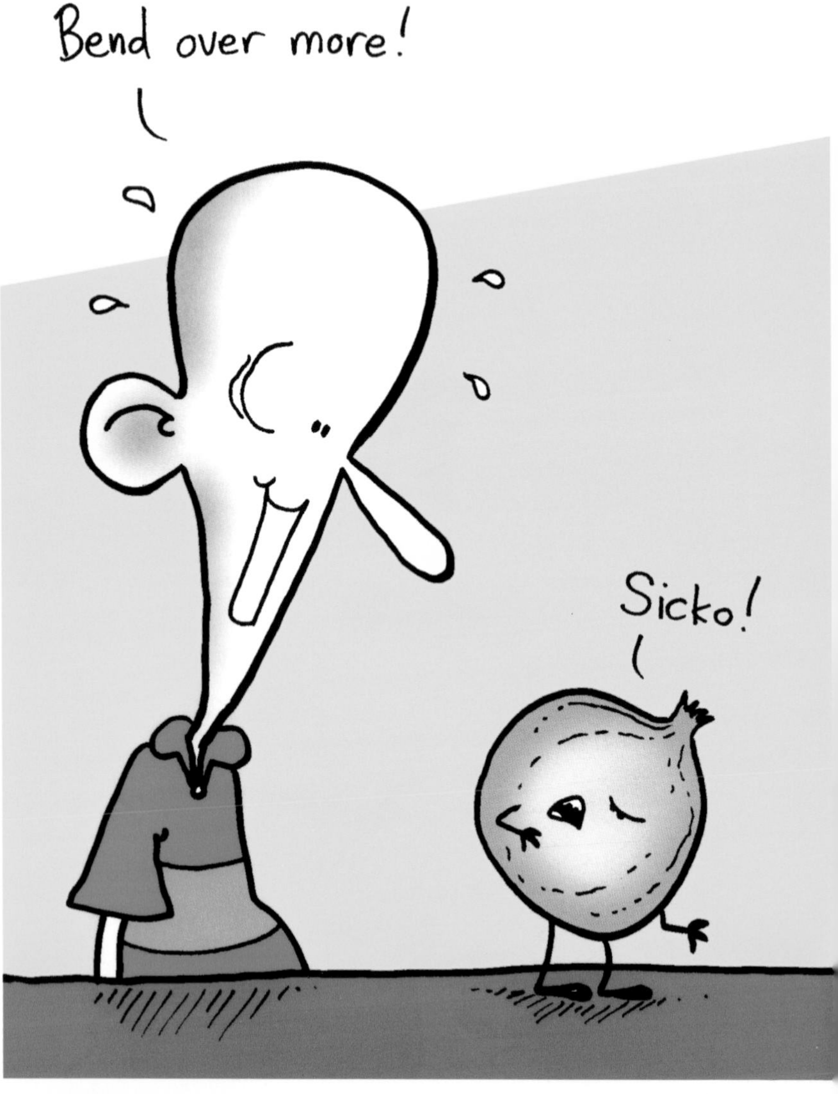

Beware of coffee machines that are out of order.

Unfortunately sex is almost impossible when she 'has the painters in'.

Never go searching for Christmas presents in your parents' bedroom.

How to stop your woman spending too much!

1. Pavlov's Dog Technique: every time she buys something, punish her.

2. Switch all her expensive make-up with disgusting alternatives.

3. Demonstrate your bank balance has hit rock bottom with the aid of a banjo.

4. As a last resort, tell her you're so skint that you have to buy non-alcoholic wine.

How you know a girl is really in love with you.

Tell your lady you're going to give her something really special on her birthday - a pearl necklace!

Always go for a pee
before making love.

Never clean your ear with a pencil near a doorway.

Why you should always ban pets
from the bedroom.

When your lady moves in with you,
you may notice a few changes.

When peeing in a phone box,
make sure it's just a quicky.

How to spot someone
having phone sex.

What kind of MAN are YOU?

THE POSER!

Spends more time in the bathroom than a woman. Would marry himself if he could.

THE NERD!

His only contact with women is through internet porn. His pants smell like a dead seagull.

Mr. SENSITIVE!

Likes the theatre, tiny animals,
listens to Coldplay and drinks
red wine (OVER 3 quid!!).
Is probably gay.

Mr. STINKY!

Whenever he starts laughing
you know he's just dropped one.
Can kill small animals with a
single pump.

When buying a new mobile, always opt for the 'poo as you go' plan.

One of the many benefits of a
poo that won't break off.

Whilst attempting to pull the old 'hole in the bottom of the popcorn box' trick, be careful who sits next to you.

How to make potato wedgies.

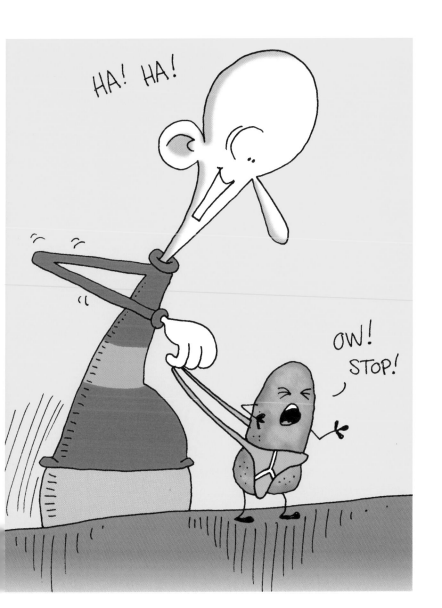

To brighten up the weekends, simply glue a pound coin onto the pavement.

There's a simple way to stop your
flatmates nicking your food - and it's free.

Thankfully there is one place you can put your remote control where no-one will touch it.

Beware: speed cameras are everywhere.

What kind of LOVER are you?

1. MR. QUICKIE - you make love in lightning fast time. Blink and she'll miss it.

2. CAPTAIN KINKY - you know every position in the book and have an arsenal of dangerous sexy toys.

3. KING OF THE OUTDOORS - you like
   the risk of being caught doing it outside.

4. THE DRUNKEN FUMBLER - you like
   to have a go even when drink has rendered
   you clinically blind.

How to make sure you never again
get a pair of socks for Christmas.

After a big curry it's best to
take precautions.

When opening the front door in your dressing gown make sure you don't have a semi sticking out.

Never trust a woman who uses sex toys.

Beware of getting oral sex from someone with a cold.

Women love waking up on their birthday to a big, sparkling ring.

Uses for an **OLD FART!**

1. FAT BUM - makes a great bouncy castle at kids parties.

2. RANCID BREATH - great for fending off burglars.

3. SAGGY BITS - ideal for storing office
   supplies and bric-a-brac.

4. EXCESS BUM HAIR - pulled taut
   makes superb violin strings!

To save money on Christmas heating bills, simply use sprout power.

Your dream woman: one who has recurring dreams of sucking big strawberry ice poles that won't go away.

Why it's best to wash your feet
before someone gives you a toe job.

Remember, women love something hard in bed.

So ... are you **GOOD** or **EVIL?**

GOOD
YOU GIVE OLD LADIES YOUR SEAT ON PUBLIC TRANSPORT

EVIL
YOU <u>USE</u> OLD LADIES AS A SEAT ON PUBLIC TRANSPORT!

GOOD
YOU DON'T MAKE A FUSS WHEN SOMEONE'S DOG MESSES YOUR LAWN

EVIL
WHEN A DOG MESSES YOUR LAWN, YOU MESS ON THE DOG!

GOOD

WHEN AN OLD PERSON FALLS YOU HELP THEM TO THEIR FEET AND GET THEM TEA

EVIL

WHEN AN OLD PERSON FALLS YOU LAUGH LOUDLY AND GATHER A CROWD

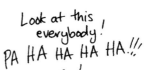

GOOD

YOU ONLY FART ALONE

EVIL

YOU ONLY FART WHEN A CHILD'S FACE IS LEVEL WITH YOUR SPHINCTER

When pushing children on swings,
always go easy.

Always keep your iPod far away from your sister's tampon packet.

Look for those tell-tale signs that someone is addicted to texting.

It's quite easy to tell when you have failed to put a nappy on properly.

If you find a worrying mole
make sure you see a doctor.

When rubbing suntan oil on your beloved
make sure you use the correct oil.

Remember - women like men who are athletic in bed.

When having a party, always clear out any old clutter to make room for the beer.

There's no better way to relax than meeting your best mates down the pub.

How to tell you're getting on a bit - your birthday cake needs a candle extension.

How to stop your computer catching viruses.

FART GALLERY

1. THE SQUEEKY

HIGH-PITCHED, LONG-LASTING, NO SMELL. COMMONLY DONE BY WOMEN.

2. THE RUMBLER

SOUNDS LIKE A DISTANT RUMBLE OF THUNDER. SMELL SEEPS OUT OVER SEVERAL HOURS. COMMONLY DONE BY OLD PEOPLE.

3. THE HOT ONE

MAKES NO SOUND BUT THE SMELL KILLS EVERYTHING IN A 12 METRE RADIUS.

4. THE RASPER

A SHORT SHARP BLAST BEST PERFORMED ON PLASTIC SEATS. GOOD FOR SCARING AWAY KIDS.

5. THE SQUELCHER

FAST UNDERWEAR CHANGE REQUIRED IMMEDIATELY!

To improve your lady's 'hand technique', simply block up the end of the ketchup bottle.

To avoid embarrassment, make sure your jazz mags are always well hidden.

How to stop your children making
a mess of your beloved car seats.

Be warned: not all kebabs are made from 100% lamb.

How *not* to get closer to the ladies.

<u>A POO</u> Spotter's Guide!

1. The TORPEDO!

DISAPPEARS AROUND U-BEND BEFORE
YOU HAVE A CHANCE TO CHECK IT OUT.
BLAST!

2. MALTESERS!

PERFECTLY ROUND AND IDENTICAL BALLS
OF FUN. WARNING: THESE POOS DO
NOT HAVE A TASTY HONEYCOMB CENTRE!

3. The CUMBERLAND!

AS IT COMES OUT, IT
CURLS AROUND TO
LOOK UP AT YOU
BETWEEN YOUR LEGS!
CREEPY!

4. The BOW TIE!

COMPLETE WITH GREEN PEA SPOTS, THIS PRETTY POO CAN BE WORN AT PARTIES!

5. The LIGHTBULB!

STARTS OFF EASY THEN...WHOAH! MAMA! TOO WIDE! TOO WIDE!!!

6. The KLINGON!

BECOMES TRAPPED IN BOTTOM HAIRS. MUST BE REMOVED WITH FINGERS, NICE.

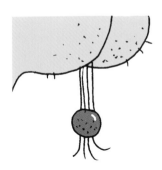

Complete your Odd Squad collection!

		ISBN	Price
The Odd Squad's Big Poo Handbook	(hardcover)	978 184161 168 6	£7.99
The Odd Squad's Sexy Sex Manual	(hardcover)	978 184161 220 1	£7.99
The Odd Squad Butt Naked		978 184161 190 7	£3.99
The Odd Squad Gross Out!		978 184161 219 5	£3.99
The Odd Squad's Saggy Bits		978 184161 218 8	£3.99
The REAL Kama Sutra		978 184161 103 7	£3.99
The Odd Squad Volume One		978 185304 936 1	£3.99
I Love Poo!	(hardcover)	978 184161 240 9	£4.99
I Love Sex!	(hardcover)	978 184161 241 6	£4.99
I Love Wine!	(hardcover)	978 184161 239 3	£4.99
I Love Beer!	(hardcover)	978 184161 238 6	£4.99
I Love Dad!	(hardcover)	978 184161 252 2	£4.99
I Love Mum!	(hardcover)	978 184161 249 2	£4.99
I Love Xmas!	(hardcover)	978 184161 262 1	£4.99
The Odd Squad's Little Book of Booze		978 184161 138 9	£2.99
The Odd Squad's Little Book of Men		978 184161 093 1	£2.50
The Odd Squad's Little Book of Oldies		978 184161 139 6	£2.99
The Odd Squad's Little Book of Poo		978 184161 096 2	£2.50
The Odd Squad's Little Book of Pumping		978 184161 140 2	£2.50
The Odd Squad's Little Book of Sex		978 184161 095 5	£2.99
The Odd Squad's Little Book of Women		978 184161 094 8	£2.99
The Odd Squad's Little Book of X-Rated Cartoons		978 184161 141 9	£2.50

HOW TO ORDER: Please send a cheque/postal order in £ sterling, made payable to 'Ravette Publishing' for the cover price of the books and allow the following for post & packing ...

UK & BFPO	70p for the first book & 40p per book thereafter
Europe & Eire	£1.30 for the first book & 70p per book thereafter
Rest of the world	£2.20 for the first book & £1.10 per book thereafter

RAVETTE PUBLISHING
Unit 3, Tristar Centre, Star Road, Partridge Green, West Sussex RH13 8RA
tel: 01403 711443   *email:* ravettepub@aol.com

Prices and availability are subject to change without prior notice.